People are talkin

"God is in this story from beginning
no problem seeing God walking with
in difficult circumstances. I think anyone reading this book will understand that giving care is an expression of love and that the ultimate source of love is God. From the purely psychological perspective, the author understands the process of adaptation resulting from the basic changes in life, the power of stress, and strategies for coping with it. She understands the role of social support, both on family and community levels. The exercises and hands-on guidelines are excellent. I recommend this book to all people who are involved in the ministry of caregiving."

Marek Wosinski, Ph.D.
Senior Lecturer, Dept. of Psychology
Arizona State University

"Pat Egan Dexter has translated her eleven-year sojourn as a caregiver into a practical and inspirational guide for others. Her courage, wisdom, and spiritual insights will take the reader from the darkness of sickness and exhaustion to the light of hope and faith."

Evan Drake Howard
Author, *Suffering Loss, Seeking Healing: Prayers for Pain-Filled Times*

"I have witnessed firsthand the challenges Pat Dexter and her husband faced and how they handled each of them. Her book accurately reflects her story and the learning curve that occurred during that period of time. The caregiver who is at the beginning of the journey will benefit greatly from her personal insight and balanced approach to care of a loved one.

Pat's experience teaches the reader the importance of relying on family members, neighbors, and one's church and community to help care for a loved one in need and also to care for oneself in the process. I will encourage my patients to read this as part of the preparation for caregiving for the terminally ill patient."

Jeanne Wolfe, M.D.
Gilbert, Arizona

"This is an easy-to-read, on-target guide written by someone who has quite obviously been there. Dexter's insights are both helpful and very user-friendly."

Charles Meyer
Author, *A Good Death: Challenges, Choices, and Care Options*
and *Surviving Death: A Practical Guide to Caring for the Dying & Bereaved*

"This book is easy to read and very engaging. The author gives of her heart to her readers, knowing how much they will need the honesty, the humor, the suggestions for coping that she offers. This will be a source of strength for husbands and wives as well as adult children who have been entrusted with the care of a loved one. It is also an excellent resource for those in the helping professions."

Sister Anna Oven, O.P.
Chaplain

"The journey of a caregiver drawn into a loved one's struggle with illness often feels like a tornado, thrusting him or her into a new world of tasks, decisions, experiences, and feelings. This ride is often accompanied by fear, loneliness, sadness, and exhaustion.

Pat Dexter is a friend to those providing friendly care, needed care, rooted in love. It is about giving care as well as receiving in very different and blessed ways. It is about deep valleys, but also those refreshing moments on the mountaintops (or at least small hills) when joy is experienced, laughter returns and hope is glimpsed."

The Rev. Fr. Richard B. Gilbert
Executive Director, The World Pastoral Care Center

"Sharing Pat Dexter's story opened my eyes to being more attentive to the needs of the caregiver. This book will be an excellent manual for training pastoral care ministers who work with long-term illness patients."

Annette Tucker, Pastoral Care Ministry
St. Tim's Catholic Community, Mesa, Arizona

Barbara D.

Coping as Caregivers

When a Loved One Is Ill

PAT EGAN DEXTER, OPL

TWENTY-THIRD PUBLICATIONS
Mystic, CT 06355

Twenty-Third Publications
185 Willow Street
P.O. Box 180
Mystic, CT 06355
(860) 536-2611
(800) 321-0411

ISBN: 0-89622-925-4
Library of Congress Catalog Card Number: 98-60128
Printed in the U.S.A.

Dedication

To those wonderful caregivers who shared their
story, so this book could be written.

Contents

Section Three – Activities & Games

Introduction

I know of no one who wants to be a full-time caregiver for a loved one. We all want those we love to be well and strong. But once the job—and it is a job—of caregiving is thrust on us, the choice is ours. Consciously or subconsciously each of us has to make a choice. Do I take it on, trust God, and do my best? Do I walk away? Do I do it reluctantly, and minimally? This is a book about strategies, about ways to make your situation as a caregiver better, easier, even more fun.

If you are a Scripture reader you know that Moses stammered, Isaiah was a man of unclean lips, Jeremiah claimed he was too young, Deborah refused to move without an army, Esther's only attribute was her beauty, Paul was blinded (as well as being despised by the other disciples), and Mary was frightened. But they all went ahead and did the job required of them. I believe the caregiver's job is just as awesome, and in a smaller way, just as important.

In addition to practical and spiritual helps this book is meant to help both the caregiver and the care receiver.

In order to make this book as helpful as possible, I compiled a questionnaire for caregivers. It was distributed at church meetings, at senior centers, and to anyone willing to share their caregiver experience.

Many responded. Some spent hours filling out the question-naire. Some responses were brief. Others would only talk to me over the phone, or in person. A few wished to be anonymous because what they confided was so private they could only share their story if no one knew who spoke.

Stories were shared in the hope you will learn and be inspired by their strategies. There is strength in knowing you do not travel this road alone. And there are constant reminders of God's gift of strength for the journey. "I can do everything through him who gives me strength" (Philippians 4:13).

Somewhere along the line the caregivers whose experiences are related said to themselves, "How can I do this better? What will work for me and my loved one?" And having said that they began to find ways. I am so grateful they were willing to share their experiences.

This book is a celebration of strategies by those who have handled "their job" with love, education, joy, and cunning. It is about what works. It also applauds those caregivers who answered "Yes" to their call.

Coping as Caregivers was created from the wisdom and experience of all those who returned the questionnaire to me, and from much other research. This book also speaks from my heart and my personal experience with a husband who, for eleven years, lived with, but was never conquered by, lymphoma—cancer of the lymph nodes.

There are ways to make the caregiver's job easier. Besides strategies, there are exercises and games—physical, mental, and spiritual. All have been tried and have worked (not all of the time, and not for all of the people, but some of the time). They have certainly been successful enough to make them worth trying. I found that my husband loved me for trying, even when something didn't work.

The book is divided into three sections. Section One has twelve short chapters. Each relates a caregiver's common experience, and the ways used to better deal with it. Each chapter ends with the strategy or strategies briefly listed.

Section Two contains guided meditations that will help the caregiver and receiver relax, communicate with God in pictures, and develop a deeper understanding of themselves and their relationship with God.

Section Three contains suggestions and specifics for spiritual, mental, and physical games and exercises.

Who am I, and what qualifies me to write this book?

Professionally, I am a teacher, a computer operator, and a writer. My sixth published book was written, for the most part, in doctors' waiting rooms, in the hospital while my husband received blood, in the x-ray center while technicians checked the progress of his disease.

My life seems to have prepared me to be a caregiver, to look for solutions. My two oldest children had asthma, severe enough so that I left Chicago for Phoenix, Arizona and relief. Although not now recommended as a solution, this worked for my children. It took about a year after we arrived in this desert climate for the attacks to subside, and for them to breathe easily.

Even my childhood seems to have been preparation for caregiving, and for finding ways to improve my caregiving skills. For this I credit my mother. Mother was a widow rearing five children under age 12 with little help. She had a cheerful nature, a belief that God would help since we were God's children as well as hers, and no matter what the circumstance, she expected us to find a better way.

During my research for this book I discovered how right my mother was. Those who used her formula of cheerfulness, work, prayer, and acceptance fared much better. They squeezed joy into their caregiving life-style.

I have always been a helper in our church, and since 1994 have proudly carried the letters O.P.L. after my name. As a lay member of the Order of Preachers (Dominicans), I serve my God and my community.

After eleven years of living with my husband's illness, I decided I had to write a book for caregivers. The idea is not just to tell you my own experiences and those of the caregivers who responded to the questionnaire, but to help you find some of the solutions in your own life, and to learn strategies for coping better.

Strategies

✧ Chapter One ✧

Self-Confidence

So we say with confidence, "The Lord is my helper; I will not be afraid. What can man do to me?"
(Hebrews 13:6)

At every age we find ourselves different persons with different life-styles. Once we were young single people with many different interests. Then many of us became newly married, with all the joys and adjustments marriage brings. Then parenthood, with all of its concerns. Usually with time we gained confidence in ourselves, in the way we handled each phase. But anxiety creeps in when we unexpectedly enter a new phase and we haven't established the rules, the habits, the norm.

When the oncologist announced, "This cancer is terminal," my confidence leaped the fence as though chased by a rabid dog. My trust in myself and in my ability to cope felt like trying to cross the freeway on foot through five o'clock traffic.

My future seemed to have disappeared with the word "terminal." The present consisted of more tests, chemotherapy, unplanned expenses, and rescheduling our lives. Married life, as I knew it, was blasted away.

In those first days Ralph's calm and confidence kept me functioning. "Don't worry. They will find a cure before it gets me," he repeated over and over. I am still ashamed when I admit my worries may have been more about myself and how I would manage than about what Ralph might endure.

Most people have someone, a family member, a special friend, in whom they can confide. Not me. Ralph had immediately sworn me to secrecy. He asked me to promise, and I foolishly agreed.

He and I talked about it, but I could not be completely open with him because I wanted to make it as easy on him as possible—which made it more difficult for me.

I tried to pretend, as did Ralph, the denial expert, that all was well. But I'm not a pretender. I am an open and talkative person. Ralph used to laugh and say, "I never worry about Pat cheating on me. She couldn't resist telling me all about it." And so with Ralph's cancer diagnosis I needed to tell all about it to someone who cared about me. But instead I kept my promise and didn't tell.

For months I told no one. During that time I developed severe headaches, and depression. Our adult children knew something was very wrong in our home. They indicated they were disappointed that we didn't trust them enough to share what it was.

Finally, my family doctor said, "Anxiety is natural in your situation, but you and Ralph must tell the children. Give Ralph a month to do it. If he refuses, you tell them. This denial, this privacy issue of his is making you sick."

Ralph refused to tell the children. So I scheduled a family dinner and told the children that we had something important to discuss. An hour before anyone arrived Ralph said, "I'll tell them."

Ralph's lighthearted joking manner when he gathered them together was akin to the way you might announce a new family puppy. "Your mother thinks," he said, "that I have cancer, and it worries her. But it's really only a little cancer. Nothing to be concerned about. It's not going to get me."

I saw the relief on the children's faces. My heart sank. Ralph may as well have denied it. And he made it sound like I overreacted.

"Let's eat," Ralph said. "Mom made a great ham roast."

Dinner was a silent affair. The children knew better than to ask him more. Privacy could have been Ralph's middle name.

After dinner our son John took me aside. "Tell me everything," he said. And I did. I was free now to share with someone who cared.

In a few days my headaches disappeared. I stopped having bouts of stomach cramps. Only then could I become open to the good parts of our life together. Only then could I keep the cancer diagnosis from constantly invading my thoughts and spoiling my life. Confidence began to return to my life. I no longer needed to sneak around and pretend. The truth had set me free, free to be myself, free to focus on honest solutions.

As time passed the children all asked me, not Ralph, what was happening about the cancer. I kept them informed, but succinctly, never dwelling on the details.

Some caregivers who responded to the questionnaire mentioned secrecy and privacy being a problem. Many mentioned difficulties after the original diagnosis. Most easily and gladly shared their situation with family and close friends. They believed, as I do, that these people have a right to know. We have a right to their comfort and compassion.

Confidence and trust are built by being truthful. Confidence comes from trying, even when we fail. Confidence grows when we face the consequences and deal with them. Confidence increases when we are flexible, and not image conscious.

Once we accept our situations, we adjust to the role of caregiver. With time, we gain confidence in ourselves and our ability to cope.

Strategies

1. Understand that anxiety is natural in the beginning of any extreme life-style change. You will learn to deal with it.

2. Be honest with those who have the right to know. Believe in yourself.

✧ Chapter Two ✧

Learn from Your Journal

*Listen to advice and accept instruction,
and in the end you will be wise.*
(Proverbs 19:20)

Almost everyone who answered the questionnaire believed the more knowledge he or she had about their loved one's particular illness the better he or she handled it. That was my experience, also.

I read every brochure the doctor gave us, every information sheet from the pharmacist, every library book about lymphoma, the immune system, what seemed to work and what didn't.

A woman I met in the doctor's waiting room said, "Educate yourself. The only thing that will cost more than an education is the lack of one." She then explained how helpful it was to keep a special journal about the progress being made.

I decided to try it. I kept a special journal just to track the illness. My journal began more as a spouting off to God about how we didn't deserve this disease.

But as the disease tried to intrude further into normal living I reported more often and with more details, keeping these reports in an easily available notebook, as one would homework assignments. Keeping a journal increased my knowledge and control.

It relieved tension to report my feelings in writing. Others affirmed this. I became more aware of the changes going on. Awareness facilitated understanding. Understanding brought calm.

I learned to use the special journal of Ralph's illness as a guide to how some medicines worked. I recorded what the doctor said, and was more knowledgeable about what to expect, and for how long. For instance, certain medicines left Ralph unable to read, but we were told that was temporary. The journal confirmed it. Sometimes solutions to specific problems would pop into my mind while writing or reading over my report. This confirmed my suspicions that God and I were working together in dealing with our situations.

Journaling also helped us understand how the disease came about. We had enough science in school to know it is a cause and effect world. So when we fell into blaming God for Ralph's illness, we had to refer back to the beginning of his cancer diagnosis and what we knew about how it had come about.

After all, hadn't Ralph and I persisted in using pesticides on the mini-farm we lived on for seven years, even after we heard much about their dangers? But using pesticides was easier than pulling weeds. We reasoned that those few chemicals couldn't possibly hurt the environment much. And who imagined it would soak into Ralph's clothing and then skin and cause cancer? Even when the sores appeared on his neck and hands Ralph ignored them until those small cancerous cells became large and deep, and malevolently moved into his bloodstream.

How dare we blame God for Ralph's cancer! Information recorded in the special journal told us about our own carelessness, our own blame.

Working with the journal also helped us to overcome fear and laziness. The great psychologist Carl Jung said that there are only two things that ever hold us back from what we want to achieve. The first is fear. The second is laziness. Both are spiritual. Both can be overcome.

Fear paralyzes, but this can be overcome by facing the thing we fear, learning about it, understanding all its components and its power. Researching and learning all you can about your particular situation will empower you, relax you, comfort you, and make you feel smarter in those helpless moments.

Laziness also paralyzes, but in a different way, by allowing lethargy to overcome desire. Laziness, lethargy can be overcome by the inner pictures our desires produce. When you wish for something, and then you picture it happening over and over again, a force is set in action. Energy comes. You are suddenly alert to possibilities, ways to make your wish happen.

The journal kept Ralph and me aware. We faced our fears. We set goals in writing, and we energized the goals with pictures in our minds of the end result.

I attended a caregivers' group that talked a lot about what to do when we reached burnout, that state of exhaustion, of no more energy. Many of my questionnaire responses spoke of this dearth of energy before the end of responsibility.

When I reached the burnout stage I read from prior entries in my journal: "...then I got a second wind," or "suddenly energy returned," or "as I prayed I gained the strength and insight to go on for however long I needed to."

I noticed the same or similar remarks about renewed energy from other caregivers. What a relief to know this. From Exodus 3:2, we remember that Moses saw a burning bush that was not being burnt out or consumed. God spoke from that bush. God is an inexhaustible source of energy. We can partake of it. My journal and others' responses confirmed this again and again.

Other caregivers and I leaned on the Lord and drew from God's energy source. I started every day on my knees praying for strength, wisdom, and mercy. I took my puny strength and plugged into the inexhaustible burning bush of God's grace.

Journaling helped me examine my feelings about our situation. This kept me from being angry at the wrong person or at the wrong time. The journal helped me discover if my feelings were controlling me, or if I controlled them. Feelings are fleeting. Like a moth racing to a light bulb, feelings can be senseless. I never wanted my feelings to control me. Writing them down allowed me to vent them, and then I decided how I would rationally handle things.

I checked my journal to see if my actions were based on emotion. Reading about my behavior educated me about myself. I often thought that if education were as attractive as sin everyone would indulge.

Strategies

1. *Learn everything possible about your situation. Have a separate notebook to report to yourself all the happenings with this illness, especially side effects of medicine and how long these lasted.*

2. *Record your moods, and they will be easier to control. Act based on valid information, using fair play and a pleasant manner. It pays.*

✧ Chapter Three ✧

Free the Child Within

And he said: "I tell you the truth, unless you change and become like little children, you will never enter the kingdom of heaven."
(Matthew 18:3)

Unless you have been a playful adult, becoming a caregiver or receiver will require an attitude adjustment. You will need to accept more of the fun of childhood. You will need to free your mind and body from many of the restrictions enforced by our society. What really is wrong with painting faces on wooden tulips, or visualizing your second grade teacher pasting a gold star on your forehead?

So cry when you feel like it, and carry tissues. Enter into the fun of experimenting with new ways of doing things. Play games. See Section Three of this book for many suitable games and activities. Be willing to laugh and fail at these games. But remember, failure is impossible because you have succeeded simply by entering into the challenge.

One of the first things we girl scout leaders were taught was that we must enter into the joy of childhood with our girls. This allowed them to feel free not to act so adult and stifled. When I danced around the floor, and oohed and aahed at Santa Claus, and covered my eyes in horror at the sight of Frankenstein on Halloween, I not only caused the girls to laugh, I laughed myself. I learned to love being a scout leader as much because of the fun as for the good I hoped would come from it.

One of the complaints my questionnaire respondents mentioned was that some of the receivers thought many of the exercises at adult day care centers were too childish. Yet for others these same exercises were fun. They delighted in talking to their toes. So my advice to both caregiver and receiver is to please allow the child in you to run free. Although your body may be bound, your spirit need not be.

We truly exist on two levels at the same time. We have the outer level where we work, play, care for what is important to us. This part of us can be seen and judged. Sometimes we are so immersed in this level we forget to let go of it and relax. But we must.

More important is the inner level, that deep and quiet place where we pray, think, resolve, and know ourselves as no one except God knows us.

Both levels are important. At the inner level we can step back from our outer challenges and relax. With God's help we learn that all is really well, that we are connected by love with a higher power, a better way. The inner level is where God allows us to create our needed and desired energy.

One way we can access this inner level is through deep breathing. Whenever fear or confusion grab your mind, snatch it back. Begin deep breathing to calm yourself. Detach from the outer level. This should only take a few seconds, but will reap hours of benefits because of better decisions.

Few of those who responded to the questionnaire mentioned deep breathing, but 80% used some form of physical exercise to relieve stress and open themselves to relaxation.

Strategies

1. Please allow the child inside yourself to run free by experimenting with different play therapy and mind and body games.

2. Use deep breathing for instant relaxation and some form of physical exercise to relieve stress regularly.

✧ Chapter Four ✧

Focus & Stay Positive

Finally, brothers, whatever is true, whatever is noble,
whatever is right, whatever is pure, whatever is lovely,
whatever is admirable—if anything is excellent or
praiseworthy—think about such things.
(Philippians 4:8)

Although some guidebooks for caregivers advise not relinquishing one's own life-style, those who answered the questionnaire all found this impossible—as did I. We full-time caregivers didn't somehow miraculously fit caregiving into our schedule; it became an important focus of our lives. Just as a new baby changes your life forever, so does becoming a caregiver for a loved one.

This book is not meant to demean the value of the good paid caregiver. I know the value of their efficiency, schedules, and common sense. Their worth is legendary. And I learned much from them. But this book was written from the viewpoint of love first. And most of us know that love makes different decisions. Love will throw away a schedule, and your sleep. Love has unseen strength and wisdom and tolerance that defies common sense. The actions triggered by love are never middle ground. Lovers relinquish. Lovers refocus.

Because I love my husband, and I love myself, my initial response to his cancer diagnosis was anger and fear.

Because my husband loved me, as well as himself, he initially responded with denial. "It won't get me," he reassured me.

Because we love God and believe God loves us, faith and hope held us in God's embrace.

Upon leaving the doctor's office after his diagnosis, my hus-

15

band Ralph said, "I may have cancer, but cancer doesn't have me." The theme of Ralph's entire eleven-year struggle with non-Hodgkin's lymphoma was his refusal to allow cancer to dictate our lives. The cancer changed our lives. We refocused. But it did not dictate our responses to life.

Somehow Ralph managed a magical dichotomy of taking whatever treatment the doctor deemed necessary to keep the cancer in check, or slam it into remission, yet never accepting that it would eventually kill him.

Ralph accepted a changed diet, chemotherapy, less energy. One of the emotional strategies Ralph used was that he never spoke of his illness to anyone except his health care workers who needed the information, and the few family members whom he felt had the right to know. Even with these individuals he never belabored it, never gave details, never complained. His responses were succinct, often humorous, and rarely negative.

I, being his wife (and half-Italian by descent), felt the right and need to cry, and carry on, and worry. "How will I ever…?" Ralph would sometimes be patient with me about this, sometimes not. But he never allowed my fear to eat away at his hope and trust. "They will find an answer, a cure," he would say. "You will find a way to cope."

When I needed to rave on about the awfulness of it all I had a friend, Mary Cooper, who gave me permission to do this. When Mary wasn't around I went to a caregivers' group, or cancer support group. This helped me. But I did not fill our home and family life with the lurid details of the illness and its treatments. I confined my lamenting to one friend or the support group.

Ralph was grateful for the nurses who joked with him and complimented or noticed him and his sense of humor and good nature. It's hard to imagine how tedious it would have been to sit as an outpatient with an IV in the arm for 2 to 4 hours three times a week without the smiles and teasing of the nurses. The glass of juice and, yes, even the choice of flavors brought smiles and sighs of another little bit of comfort, another small joy because the nurses were so considerate.

Often, when we came home after a treatment, and before he would lie down for a much needed nap, Ralph would recount to me all the nice things done for him. Sometimes he would mention the soft chairs, so much easier on his bony bottom, or the bright plants which he was sure were there to clean the air. I hadn't noticed all these things. I was buried in my book. But soon I began to intentionally notice the good stuff and remark on it. It became a bit of a game to see who could notice which good thing first, or what the other had missed.

For us this searching for good things became a great upper, a positive strategy for helping life to be better. By deciding to be grateful we made it a point to detail and remark about the good things.

Many who responded to the questionnaire mentioned how depressing it was to talk so much about the illness. They didn't object so much to the time and energy spent on treatment as to the constant questions and focus on the illness, rather than on some of the other good things in life.

Family, friends, even bare acquaintances, usually meaning to be kind, seemed to think it was important to ask about the health of the loved one. But, too often, they got into the habit of asking about nothing else. The ill person was labeled "Jake, with the cancer" or "Paula, whose mother has Alzheimer's." All this focus on illness was a downer for both the caregiver and the receiver.

I found myself making a special point of saying, "Thanks for asking. We're plugging along. But let me tell you about...(this good thing that happened, or what I saw...)." Before long the well-meaning ones caught on and realized there was more to our life than the illness.

A number of those responding to the questionnaire mentioned they also had to deal with other family members who resented the time given to the receiver. One respondent confided that her husband was angry with her because she took care of her mother. He said it wasn't the caregiving that bothered him as much as the constant talk of it. He wanted more attention paid to him. She soon learned to set aside a special time for him in which the focus was on their relationship. But others were angry and upset that they received criticism rather than support. How to handle this will be addressed further in another chapter.

Life changes. Focus realigns itself. Learn to focus on the positive, on possibilities, on hope, and on the love you feel for each other.

Strategies

1. Follow doctor's orders, but speak about the illness only to health care workers, and the few family members who have a right to know.

2. During visits for treatments notice as many nice and comfortable things as possible: the consideration shown by nurses, the plants, the sweet coolness of the orange juice, the good humor among patients.

✧ Chapter Five ✧

Gradually

*A time to search and a time to give up, a time to keep
and a time to throw away.*
(Ecclesiastes 3:6)

After my husband's diagnosis, our family doctor, Jeanne Wolfe, said to me, "Begin now to share the driving so that when Ralph can no longer drive he will have become used to your driving him. Then he won't suddenly be faced with another loss of his powers."

Easier said than done. As with so many post-World War II couples, he drove whenever we went somewhere together. The first time I mentioned that I planned to drive us home from the doctor's, his lips protruded like a shelf. The pout on his face said, "I will not let you drive me home like you drove our children." "I can do it," he griped.

"I know you can, Ralph. But so can I. And I want to start sharing the driving with you."

"No." He closed his mouth in determination. As soon as we left the doctor's office Ralph pulled out his car keys, and hurried to the car. He jammed his thinning body into the driver's seat like General MacArthur taking back the Philippines. No stopping him this time. I smiled and slid into the passenger's side.

On the ride home I explained patiently that Dr. Wolfe suggested we start now to share the driving.

He shook his head. "When I can't drive, you can," he declared. We drove home in silence.

The next week when we left the doctor's office I got into the driver's seat before he did. He fussed at me and refused to get into the car until I got into the passenger's seat. After a few minutes I moved over, but not before I explained again, with love and truth, that I was going to start driving home from the doctor's. He didn't answer. He was satisfied for now that he was in the driver's seat.

But the next time I persisted in getting to the driver's seat ahead of him, and the time after that I didn't move over. He stood outside the car. "I don't like your driving. It makes me nervous."

"That's okay," I replied. "I don't always like your driving either. Come on, honey, get in and let's go home."

He did. He was tired and full of medicine from the chemotherapy treatments. He grumbled all the way home. But he was intelligent enough to know it was the right decision.

Gradually I drove more; he drove less. At times he was angry with my driving, his weakness, the traffic. But we faced the loss of his driving ability together. Whenever he was able he drove to the doctor's office.

I personally found I had to cast aside my tender feelings and ignore some of the insults that came from my angry husband. I had to open my heart and mind and understand how difficult it must be for him to be the needy one—a man who had always been such a good caretaker to our family.

I tried, always, to remind him that love is fair, and it was only fair that he be cared for now. We always held onto hope that his body would recover from this cancer assault, that he would be restored. Certainly he would be restored in heaven if not on earth (though we preferred earth and now).

At times I was tempted to lie to relieve my loved one's stress, but didn't because I knew my Lord wouldn't like it. I looked at whatever was happening in a positive light, but never lied about his actual condition. My husband told me he appreciated always receiving the truth, even when it hurt. So the truth was always kinder.

Sharing the driving got easier. He finally accepted that I wasn't trying to take over, but rather to ease into the inevitable.

Gradually, and with much persistence and patience, with truth as your guide, and God's strength as part of your own, take over what you must. Like a person whose eyes go from regular glasses to bi-focals to cataract surgery we all must accept help as needed. Generally we are very grateful to get it.

This idea of taking over gradually was a strategy used by many caregivers who understood the reluctance of the receiver to give up control. We respected their anger and defiance. But we persisted in honesty and love. Most of the time, "gradually" the transition came about.

Strategies

1. Whenever possible, make changes gradually. If at all possible do it before the actual need arises.

2. In truth and honesty, always explain why you are doing this. Explain kindly and as often as necessary, trying to imagine how you might feel if you faced this loss.

✧ Chapter Six ✧

Ways to Pray

"If you believe, you will receive whatever you ask for in prayer."
(Matthew 21:22)

Prayer was the most important strategy I used to get through those eleven years of caregiving as my husband battled cancer.

At certain times only a particular type of prayer worked for me. I do not believe there is a wrong way to pray. But there are many different ways to pray, conversations with God, music, ritual or rote prayers, silent song prayers, sometimes referred to as a mantra, that are repeated over and over and over which give peace and spiritual strength. I will detail a bit about each type of prayer as well as why and how that particular type worked for me at that time.

Conversational prayer has always been my favorite way to pray. These prayers usually begin with just thinking about God and how his presence in my life brings blessings. Then I find myself speaking to the Lord as I would a good friend, or a lover.

Sometimes conversational prayer begins when I am reading Scripture. I begin to talk to God, usually silently, about how this particular passage touches me, or teaches me. But often conversational prayer springs from my mind. "God, what should I do?" Or, "God, I love you for sending this rain." Or, "God, please help me be kinder to Aunt Matilda. You know she makes me crazy." Or, "God, I'm so scared right now. Hold me closer."

Even though conversational prayers have been my favorite, in certain crises only ritual or rote prayers worked.

When I was in labor with my first child any conversation I had with God might have been combative. Remembering what the nun taught me in school I repeated the Lord's Prayer over and over again. Wonder of wonders a peace finally came over me. Pain subsided to the back of my mind and, relaxed and trusting, three hours later I was delivered of a beautiful baby girl. I am so grateful for ritual or rote prayers. I could not have concentrated on any other type of prayer at that time.

During some of the worst times of my husband's illness, I could only communicate with God through short phrases which I referred to as silent songs—a repeating of a short phrase, sacred words, or Scripture.

One night Ralph reached over to my side of our king-size bed. This usually gentle man woke me with a shaking. He was coughing blood and unable to speak. Why I didn't call 911 I will never know. Instead I began a silent song prayer, pulled on my clothes, grabbed my car keys, and helped Ralph to the car. We live five minutes from the hospital emergency room. I got him into the emergency room and under a doctor's care within seven minutes of being awakened. It was the right thing to do. They had all the needed resources to help him.

Not one word had been spoken between Ralph and me or the doctors and me. No words were needed. But I had begun my inner song the second I saw Ralph's distress. "He leads me through troubled waters," my mind repeated over and over and never stopped until Ralph rested comfortably in the hospital bed. Then, as I relaxed, my inner song changed to "The Lord is my strength and my song." Finally I felt God's peace encircling me. The crisis had passed. These inner songs kept me focused on God, instead of on the trouble. Trust in God increased. No amount of careful planning will ever replace God's grace.

Musical prayers seemed to work best at times when I was doing routine chores around the house, or feeling a little sorry for myself, or riding in the car to shop. Those tapes of popular Christian music kept my mind tuned to God and all God's blessings, rather than allowing my mind to wander into worry or frustration. It was my experience that keeping my inner mind tuned to God helped me function better on the outer material level.

Grace came on its own.

Many who responded to the questionnaire had similar experiences. Those who had regularly prayed reported more peace of mind, more trust in God's presence, more acceptance. Mostly, they believed God would somehow make something good of all this. Some of these caregivers felt, as I do, that going to church often was a great source of strength. For me daily Mass and communion forged the steel into my spine. Many Catholic Christians spoke of the comfort Mass and communion gave them.

Those who began to pray only after problems arose seemed more drained emotionally. Fear and strain cut into them like climbing a rocky mountain in bare feet.

Those who had been praying regularly also felt as if they were climbing a mountain. But regular prayer prepared them, like having mountain boots broken in and ready for the climb.

I believe prayer should be a first resort, not the last. Pray first. Ask for what you need. Don't wait, as so many did, until you are sore and bleeding, until your own resources are depleted.

Go to the Lord with open hands, naked, weak, and vulnerable. Admit that without God you can do so little. Ask God to stick to you like gum on a shoe, to be there with and in every decision.

Picture prayers, also called meditations, worked well for me when I needed help falling asleep. The second section of this book details a number of meditations for fun and imaginative walks with God.

Of course, any time you go to God in prayer is the right time. And almost all who prayed at any time and in any way believed it helped.

Every day, as you wake, admit how much you need God. And every night before you go to sleep say "thank you" to the unseen one who carried you through another day.

God understands. There is nothing you can suffer that God didn't suffer. Jesus went constantly to his father for help. He wants us to include him.

Prayer, being open to God, is a way of being enveloped with God's grace. I noticed that often spiritual gifts come before physical or material ones. Because of prayer, I felt a peace before my loved one was comforted. Because of prayer, I was more patient when nothing seemed better. Because of daily prayer, I trusted in the Lord. I felt hope energizing my soul, and fear was kept at bay.

Strategies

1 . Get into the habit of daily prayer. Don't wait until trouble starts. Every day as you wake admit how much you need God. And every night before you go to sleep say "thank you" to the unseen one who carried you through another day.

2. Fit the type of prayer to the occasion. Sometimes conversational prayers are best, sometimes rote or ritual prayers, sometimes music, sometimes only a silent song prayer will work.

✧ Chapter Seven ✧

Respite and Depending on Others

*"Come to me, all you who are weary and burdened,
and I will give you rest."*
(Matthew 11:28)

It's a mistake to act as though the salvation of this person you are caring for depends entirely on you. It does not. There are many forces at work. We caregivers must lean on others: doctors, hospitals, friends, church, and most of all God. But sometimes all the help is for the sick one. Caregivers forget about their personal needs. One can only give so much without breaking, or at least tilting.

Once I passed beyond the shock of the initial diagnosis, I adjusted and managed to handle things fairly well. I thought I always would. Then, after we passed our tenth year of dealing with the cancer, I suddenly found myself so weary I wanted to die. My life-style had become too burdensome for me. I felt like I was sinking into a pit. In fact I was having dreams of being locked in a small dark room with a deep pit in the center of the floor. I wanted to get away from it.

During my waking hours I was losing energy, something I usually have in abundance. None of these burdens was imaginary. By this time Ralph's treatments and side effects were constant. He got better, then worse, then better, then worse, then better, then worse again. The doctors could keep him from dying, but they couldn't make his body well enough to do anything beyond feeding himself and keeping himself clean. All the chores fell on me, most of the physical taking care of him, all of the cleaning and upkeep of the home, and even the family finances.

I believed the quality of our life was at 0 to minus 1. Ralph didn't agree. His mind was good and clear. He enjoyed watching television and visits with friends. He could play cards for a few hours one evening a week, providing he slept until game time. When he was awake and not under treatment he was still good company. But oh, what a burden this all was to me.

The dreams were a warning to me. I found myself wanting it all to end, wanting to run away, something. Never before had I cried over a missing button, or a phone number dialed incorrectly. Now everything made me snappish. The family sat back and quietly hoped I would find a solution. They kept saying, "Mother is so strong, so capable." And they busied themselves with their own lives.

Finally I reached out to my church. I called Sr. Anna, the one at St. Timothy's parish who is in charge of helping the chronically ill. I wasn't sure if this was the right thing to do since my chronically ill husband had everything he needed. I was the one in trouble.

"Is there anything for me?" I asked Sr. Anna.

"Oh, yes," Sr. Anna said. "We understand and recognize your problem, too." She first suggested a caregivers' support group to air my feelings. Then she told me of a Catholic program run by the diocese called Foundation for Senior Living where I could get help with the cost on a sliding economic scale. They had respite care. It was suggested I should get away about three times a week for play therapy.

I took the help offered. I tried a few caregivers' support groups before I found just the right one for me. When one group facilitator's first suggestion was to get my doctor to give me drugs for depression, I looked elsewhere. If your doctor thinks you need medication, I would not speak against this. But I didn't like it as a first resort. And I found my respite without anti-depression drugs.

The caregivers' support group I chose immediately eased any guilt I felt about being resentful and angry about my burden. Also, I was given many hints to make the job easier. This group talked a lot about acceptance, and some basic changes in my behavior.

For instance, I arranged for Ralph to take Dial A Ride, a transportation program the city runs so disabled or elderly people can get to their doctor and treatment appointments.

Ralph didn't like this change. He preferred that I continue to do all the transporting and waiting for him. But I insisted that I needed to lighten the backpack of his appointments. He never liked the idea. He grumbled a lot about it. But gradually he understood and cooperated.

A few times a week I went to the Senior Center and played games (never mind that I didn't think I was old enough to be there). I found this helped get my energy back. It's called play therapy, and everyone needs some. Once I signed up for a two-day escorted river rafting trip. Then I asked our son David if he would look after his father for those two days. David cheerfully agreed. In most of my requests for help I found being specific about what I needed, and having a set time brought much more cooperation. I spoke briefly, but clearly. A vague request or complaint brought a vague response, or none at all.

I still had the same situation. But now I didn't feel so burdened by it. My husband didn't like some of the changes, but none of them hurt him or cheated him in any way. So it's okay if he didn't like it that he had to sit in a comfortable chair in an air-conditioned office and wait a half hour for his ride home. That's better than my sitting next to him for 2 to 3 hours in the treatment room, and feeling resentful.

My dreams of falling into the pit disappeared. I again accepted my situation, but I also reached out, learned what was available to me, and made use of it.

Jesus carried his cross up that hill, but he allowed Simon of Cyrene to help him.

Most of those who responded to the questionnaire used respite, particularly when the caregiving went on and on. At first there was some guilt, but soon energy returned along with a more cheerful outlook, which overcame any uneasy feelings.

Strategies

1. As soon as you notice you are becoming snappish and depressed get help and make some changes in your schedule. If family won't help, contact your church or Social Services.

2. Be specific with what help you need and for how much time. Before using prescription drugs for depression, try prayer, meditation, fist-in-the-pillow therapy, and asking for specific time-outs.

Chapter Eight

Handling Criticism

We want to avoid any criticism of the way
we administer this liberal gift.
(2 Corinthians 8:20)

One of the questions my questionnaire asked was: In order of emotional impact, what were the three most hurtful things said or done?

Some of the respondents mentioned the criticism they received. This hurt emotionally because they felt the job of caregiving was hard enough without being put down. Criticism of the caregiver is not uncommon. I have always wondered at how sensitive we can be to the mosquito-sized remarks of relatives, yet capable of withstanding elephant-sized comments from strangers.

Sometimes, out of their confusion and fear, the criticism came from the care receivers. This seemed to wound the deepest.

At times the person being cared for seemed to take delight in embarrassing the caregiver. A once good-natured mother would publicly accuse her daughter of hurting her. A once shy and faithful husband would proposition the waitresses whenever they went to a restaurant.

There were many misinformed but judgmental statements like, "I don't think you are keeping Mother happy enough." "Mother says you are spending too much of her money."

Many responded that unkind words not only bruised the ego, they caused the caregivers to doubt themselves. One example:

For over two years Sarah had been taking care of her husband

Milton. Milton was in his 70s with a disabled leg and then a heart attack. Then he began having small strokes which left his usual bright and cheerful self confused and often angry. Sarah received some help from their adult son, but no help from Milton's family of origin.

One day, after listening to their brother Milton's complaints his two sisters decided Sarah wasn't doing a good job taking care of Milton. They told her so.

Sarah was emotionally crushed. She checked with Milton's doctors (he had three). She checked with Home Health Care (Milton had refused to cooperate with them). And she checked her calendar (a good part of the day was taken up with Milton's needs). Then Sarah checked with her conscience. It was clean, clear, and ready for sainthood, she decided.

Sarah then suggested privately to each sister-in-law that she could take over Milton's care if she wanted it—"Or no more complaints," Sarah said.

Neither sister-in-law wanted Milton's care. The complaints still came in offhand remarks and innuendoes, but Sarah cheerfully dismissed those as one might junk mail.

Don't let anyone downgrade you. Make sure especially that you don't put yourself down. You are a person of value. If you do something stupid, don't tell yourself you are stupid. Tell yourself "that was a stupid action. I'll do better next time." Best not to worry about what other people might think. Concern yourself with what God would think of it. If we're okay in God's eyes, we're okay, even if some of our actions could use improvement.

As caregivers we often find ourselves at a crossroads time of life, without an option as to which road to take. We must look and listen for positive ways to live in the moment. But sometimes, without meaning to be hurtful, others make that difficult. Do your soul a kindness and forgive them, for they know not what they do.

Strategies

1 . Believe in yourself, but also check criticism for truth and help-ful ideas. Pass off and forgive ignorant remarks.

2. Take aside the one who criticized, and offer that person the caregiving job. Be ready to relinquish all or part of the work. (It will never happen.)

✧ Chapter Nine ✧

Grateful or Hateful

*...sing psalms, hymns and spiritual songs
with gratitude in your hearts to God.*
(Colossians 3:16)

Some of those who responded to the questionnaire reported how difficult it is to have all one's efforts taken for granted. No apparent gratitude left them feeling frustrated.

Do we hear this same frustration in Jesus' voice when he says to the one cleansed leper who returned to thank him, "Were not all ten cleansed? Where are the other nine?" (Luke 17:17).

Wouldn't it seem logical that the greater the need the more grateful the person would be? From some of the responses I received it doesn't seem to be the case.

Sometimes the care receiver behaves in a mean way. When the unwarranted and cruel words come, it becomes the responsibility of the caregiver to know it was the pain talking, or the frustration raging. Most of the time it has nothing personally to do with the caregiver.

I suggest you listen to the tirade, to what is being said, and when you have gleaned enough information and insight from the outburst (and you will if you are listening for the other's feelings, and not just responding with your own), place this tirade in an imaginary bubble, seal it with a kiss, and allow it to float away into the world where it will dissipate without harm.

Don't let hurtful and hateful words slap away your comfort zone. Ugly words can sit on your heart like an elephant on your chest. Let those words slide off, like the soap after you shower. Clear it away. You need a free heart and all your energy for the worthwhile work you are doing.

Consider Beth and Bill (not their real names). Bill has a heart condition that so weakened him he could no longer work. The medication he had to take left him nauseated. Bill, once a capable family provider, felt useless, worthless. He leaned on Beth for almost everything, and he had become verbally abusive to her. Because he was angry at his situation he withheld his gratitude as a way of feeling some power in his life.

Beth did not handle this well. At first she returned his verbal abuse, then withdrew and did barely what was necessary for his survival. This increased his verbal abuse and ridicule of her. She knew that if she didn't learn how to deal with it she would have to leave him. Beth truly did not want to do this. They had been married nearly forty years. The children loved their father, and seemed to feel sorry for him without thinking about how his verbal abuse affected her.

Beth wisely sought counseling. Bill refused to cooperate with this so she went alone. She asked the counselor, "Doesn't he know how hard this is for me? Why can't he be a little grateful instead of being so mean?" And she listened and learned.

The next time Bill became verbally abusive Beth told him, "I am a valuable person to you. And I love you. I have feelings, too. Your gruff manner offends me. If you ever loved me you should be more considerate in the way you speak to me." Bill did not reply.

With the help of the counselor, Beth discovered she had three choices. She could leave. She could learn how to live with it. She could ignore it completely.

Trying to ignore it was almost impossible for Beth. It increased Bill's need for attention and using verbal abuse was one way he got it.

Once Beth determined that she would not leave Bill, she opened her mind to ways to handle it so nobody would lose. First Beth learned to stop expecting Bill's gratitude. She also learned not to give in to any of his unreasonable demands. With help from the counselor Beth set her own agenda as to what she believed was the right way to handle the situation. She acted instead of reacting.

Beth willingly and pleasantly did all that was needed to help Bill with his health problems. But she refused to respond to verbal abuse, and she found a few hours a week for respite. The situation became tolerable for her.

To Beth's surprise after a few months Bill did tell her he was grateful for all her care. Although she was glad to hear it, Beth found she no longer needed his gratitude to feel right about herself.

Why is one so grateful, and another so hateful? Certainly pride is a factor. Some think it lowers their stature to say "thank you."

Some don't want to admit how needy they are. Yet we are all needy. Even Jesus. Jesus always thanked his Father first before eating, before any miracle performed.

The refusal to acknowledge someone's gift of time, money, or energy is a way to tweak his or her nose, to irritate, to have a small power over the other. It's a way of saying, "You owe me. I'm as good as you are. Why should I acknowledge your gift? Of course, I'll take it. I need it. But I won't give you the satisfaction of knowing how much." The counselor suggested this is a sort of one-up-on-you feeling.

Sometimes gratitude is withheld because the person feels jealous that you have it to give, and they do not. But what giver wants to be taken for granted? To be expected to give? Who doesn't feel angry, or used, or, like Jesus, wonder why, when we give a gift, it is not even acknowledged?

When Ralph and I joined a group in our church that feeds the homeless every Saturday night we were told by the leader, "If you find yourself judging these people, or you expect them to be grateful, you are in the wrong ministry." Pleasantly enough we did find that about a third of the singles we served did say thank you. And of those families who came, almost all expressed gratitude.

We decided that if we gave a gift it had better be free, no strings attached, no expectations of how it would be received. If we felt that we must be appreciated for what we gave, then it was better not to give.

Yet, in a different circumstance, where there is no great need, if I give a family member a gift and that person does not respond at all, by the third gift I do not give more. I assume if it wasn't important enough to be acknowledged, then I choose not to spend my time and money getting it. I have done this even with my grown children whom I love very much. They are independent. I see no sense in putting my gifts upon them if they choose to ignore the same.

This response could not apply to my caregiving, however. As we agreed to feed the homeless, regardless of their reaction, once I agreed to be the caregiver I would do the job, gratitude or not.

When Jesus healed the ten, and only one responded, Jesus did not stop healing. God hasn't stopped the rain and the sunshine because so many take them for granted. Nor would I stop feeding and caring for my children if they were needy. Loves gives without expecting return.

But, oh, the joy and wonder of a grateful heart! I have found that when I say thanks to God, I am given even more to be thankful for—just as the one who acknowledges my gift will receive even more, if I have it to give.

So let the ungrateful one, the angry one, the jealous one, the lazy one, the selfish one tweak your nose. If I do what I believe is the right thing to do, then I am at peace with myself, and with God.

I remember the last St. Patrick's Day that Ralph and I went out to breakfast. The waitress greeted us with a big smile. She had on a silly green hat, and a shamrock on her pocket. She told us a funny joke about what you would call an Irishman who sat out all night in the backyard (Patty O'Furniture, of course). The waitress was not only funny, she was efficient and considerate. As we prepared to leave Ralph left a tip that was larger than the break-fast tab. "Why so much?" I asked.

"Because she made me laugh. She made me feel so good. I guess I'm just grateful."

How often I remembered that statement when we were going through some of our worst times. I would try to find something to make us laugh. I could always make Ralph feel good by letting him know he was so worth any trouble. "You are my husband, and I love you dearly." I told him many times. I was one of the lucky ones whose husband was grateful—most of the time.

I must admit that I, too, had been guilty of being hateful when I should have been grateful. As mentioned before, when we first heard Ralph's diagnosis, it took me weeks to get my emotions under control. I was sick in my soul. I said some mean and hurt-ful things to people who did not deserve it.

I sulked. My face drooped, and those mean words, I realize now, were devices to get my way, to get sympathy. But meanness has a way of echoing back. I hurt myself more than anyone. Doors were closed to me, and I was less effective in getting done what was needed.

So I stopped. I made a decision to handle things with infor-mation, fair play, and a pleasant manner. The doors opened again. People cooperated.

Strategies

1. Don't expect gratitude. Give freely, with no strings attached. But be glad if a "thank you" comes.

2. Act. Don't react. With the help of a counselor, you decide which demands are reasonable. Try to be good-natured to your loved one no matter how mean and undeserving they are at the time. And guard yourself from hateful actions.

✧ Chapter Ten ✧

Humor

Blessed are you who weep now, for you will laugh.
(Luke 6:21)

Let healthy humor enter in whenever possible. Healthy humor is never a putdown of the sick one, but often a small putdown on the teaser.

Those who responded to the questionnaire happily reported the effects of humor on their loved one. Playful teasing by visitors was greeted with smiles.

A kiss on the neck from an old friend and a comment about trouble finding the neck with these new glasses brought a giggle.

"Why are you in that bed when I'm so tired I could fall off this chair?" remarked one visitor. A grin and the desire to change places answered that remark.

One fellow said to a mother in a wheelchair, "Those bright and sparkling eyes know something special they aren't telling!" A smirk, and a nod of the head answered that remark. Why not? Everyone has secrets. That never changes.

One animal lover to another should always have a playful pet story to tell. For example, there's the old story about the worried man, holding a dog in his arms, waiting his turn for the bus to heaven. A priest happened by. The man stopped the priest and asked, "Father, will God allow my Peppy into heaven with me?"

The priest looked heavenward, looked at the dog, and the concern on the man's face. "Sir," he replied, "I believe God will allow all his good and faithful creatures into heaven."

Relief flooded the man's face. "Oh, thank you, Father."

The bus to heaven came. The bus to heaven pulled away and the man still stood on the corner, watching the dog on the bus wagging a good-bye.

Illness can be embarrassing. But embarrassment can often be turned into humor. An Alzheimer's spouse or relative who likes to sing out loud in public places can be shrugged away with a grin and the remark, "John (or Mother) is practicing for when he (she) takes a shower."

One respondent reported that while on the streetcar her mother sang to a handsome thirtysomething young man, "Believe Me If All Those Endearing Young Charms." The young man listened, smiled, and said, "No one has ever sung that to me before. Thank you." This respondent "learned to laugh and realize that appearances and public scenes did not matter."

Another reported that because of his thinness Dad's pants would often slip down in public, and Dad was past caring. She used belts, suspenders, and a favorite statement: "Hike! Up we go you wandering trousers!" Then she issued a grimace that would make anyone grin.

Children who witnessed this hiking up of the pants always laughed, sometimes out loud. They couldn't help it, she said. And their laughter made Dad feel good. "If I captured these on camera, I could have made a fortune on Funniest Home Videos," she said.

Many reported that children, especially after age nine, were wonderful helpers. Once you received their parents' permission, they would happily fetch wheelchairs, carry items, open doors, and explain to others that you needed to get through. Helpful children brought joy to all who watched them in action. And they seemed to feel good about themselves while they helped.

A lovely lady in her seventies told about when she and her husband had to work on his physical therapy. They called it spouse abuse.

Another woman reported that when her husband had to go into diapers they called it "the pamper patrol." Once she said to him, "Did we ever dream when we were changing our children's diapers that I would some day be changing yours, and not minding it a bit?" She received a kiss on the hand for that remark.

For some, water was a great source of fun. In Arizona, where we live, a summer rain is a rare treat. Ralph and I would stand out in it and let it fall all over us. Water is much more than a cleanser, it can be a spiritual adventure. Some splashed in the rain, wheelchair and all. Others told of sprinkling water on each other just for fun and attention. And the best water story I heard was about a foot-splashing contest. Those involved each dunked their feet in a large, soft plastic pan of water and went at it on the patio to see who could get the other the wettest.

Have you ever heard the story of the twin babies in the womb? It was getting very crowded and uncomfortable in there, and somehow they knew it was almost time for birth. One twin sighed mightily and said to the other, "Do you think there really is life after birth?"

I really think so. And I think there is fullness of life while waiting for the inevitable. So much joy, so many funny stories, so much hope and playfulness. So many people cannot be wrong.

Find something to laugh about every day. There is something to enjoy each and every day: the food is good. This TV program is fun. Your company is delightful. When I am clean it makes me feel special and important.

Find someone or something to compliment someone about: I appreciate your being on time. Your smile fills my joy center. Your cooking is good, great, terrific.

Strategies

1. Use lighthearted playful remarks, gentle putdowns on self while visiting. Have a humorous remark ready for those public embarrassing moments. See the Games and Exercises section of this book.

2. After receiving parents' permission, ask children to help fetch wheelchairs, open doors, carry items, and be a temporary angel for you. Most will do it lovingly.

✧ Chapter Eleven ✧

The Calendar

*He replied, "Go into the city to a certain man and tell him,
'The Teacher says: My appointed time is near.'"*
(Matthew 26:18)

The appointed time is a most important part of what you do as a caregiver.

At the beginning of each month we marked the calendar. Treatment days. Social times. Projects we hoped to do around the house, or taking the car in for service.

From the beginning of our marriage, like many other couples, we had kept a calendar to set appointments and schedule projects. While rearing three children who all had different activities it seemed the only way to keep our life in order. And it helped set priorities. Once the children left the calendar continued at a more relaxed pace.

With the onset of Ralph's treatments all our priorities were realigned. Cancer treatment times went on the calendar first and were a first priority. Sometimes one entire week of the month was scheduled for this. We always allowed for three days after chemotherapy for Ralph's strength to return. But even on those days we were prepared for a card game, and television viewing.

The calendar was a stress reliever. We looked at those nothing-scheduled days as pure gift. If Ralph's strength allowed we would take walks. If not, a long game of cards or a quick game of Aggravation would always be available to us.

We also went to events listed in the paper now without waiting for out-of-town guests to request them. The zoo, always a favorite with us, was a ride around on the zoomobile. Movies were always on tap at home courtesy of our VCR.

I had a private list for times when I needed to get away. Ralph wasn't selfish. He understood we had different energy levels and interests. I had my personal list I could do for a few hours. I planned a retreat with my church group twice a year. I didn't always make it, but the planning and hoping were always fun. And just having it on the calendar gave me hope. As time went on our son David offered to look in on his Dad while I "retreated."

We had to have a flexible attitude about the calendar and the lists. They were a starting point, a place of hope. But we made whatever changes were necessary without grumbling. We had an attitude of gratitude that Ralph was still around. It was our decision to laugh and joke about the problems. God was part of our experience.

We had hoped to go to China someday. We knew we wouldn't be doing it in this world so we imagined ourselves holding hands and traveling together as spirits, exploring China. It was great fun. We saw the Great Wall on video and in our minds. We saw it from the clouds, and in our minds. God is mystery. He gave us imagination to make our lives better. Why not imaginary travel?

It was our private fun trip. The children were overjoyed to find us having secrets, private jokes, as when we were young. Life might not be perfect, but it was good. God said so. God saw all that he had done and called it good.

Strategies

1. Mark all appointments on the calendar. Include recreation and retreat times. Consider days with nothing scheduled as pure gift. The calendar frees our mind and transfers responsibility. It allows you to comfortably say "No."

✧ Chapter Twelve ✧

Accepting the Unchangeable

*...to accept his lot and be happy
in his work—this is a gift of God.*
(Ecclesiastes 5:19)

Acceptance means behaving in a loving way toward the one you are caring for. You must already be doing this, or you wouldn't be reading this book.

Acceptance doesn't mean passive care. It means educating yourself to know all you can about this illness, what is normal, what to expect, and the choices of help available to you so you can deal with it.

Acceptance means believing and communicating to your loved one that he or she is worth the effort, the work. Let him or her know that you are in this together for as long as it takes.

Our world may never reach the level of our wishes, but when we aggressively accept, and work at making it better, it will be a better world for us and our loved one.

Acceptance of your situation will be like oil sprayed on squeaking hinges. The inner peace that comes with acceptance will smooth your feelings like cream rubbed into dry hands.

Acceptance means loving yourself more because you have agreed to unconditionally love and help someone else.

Acceptance is knowing what you have the right to control, and doing it.

Acceptance is learning what you cannot control, like someone else's feelings, and leaving it alone.

Acceptance comes more easily when, although we may not

understand the why or all that is going on, we trust God to be in all of it with us.

All of us caregivers discovered there is always something we can do to ease our agony. Peace of mind comes when we understand and accept where we are now.

As mentioned earlier all caregivers accepted their role. For the most part we emerged from the experience stronger, smarter, kinder, and more confident of ourselves than we ever dreamed possible.

We who survived the caregiving voyage know how Columbus felt when land was again beneath his feet. We who carried our small lighted candle into the dark tunnel and came out at the end found a new dawn of knowing what joy is. We now understand. We have experienced the energy from God's burning bush.

The end of Ralph's and my journey came in the way Ralph hoped. And I will never forget the brightness shining from his blue eyes, or the smile on his face.

Ralph had asked if he could stay home and be cared for. I promised that if it was humanly possible for me, he would have his wish.

When the doctor said "three months maximum left," Ralph, for reasons of his own, refused the hospice care offered to us. It would have been easier on me, but because of his private nature he just didn't want "strangers," kind as they were, milling around.

With the doctor's advice I enlisted the services of Home Health Care. Ralph accepted this. He had no choice. A nurse came for about an hour every day, and a social worker took care of any equipment needed. She also checked on my well-being. I bathed Ralph, fed him when he couldn't feed himself, and stayed within voice reach.

In the last days I could barely get him to the bathroom. One night he fell. It was a terrible strain to get him up and into bed again. When the visiting nurse came the next day she said, "During the day we can get help to you in five to ten minutes. But not at night. If you are keeping him at home, you will now need a person to sleep over, a strong male to carry him and pick him up when he falls."

I shook my head, more from confusion than refusal. So many of those who responded to the questionnaire indicated that even though their loved one's mind was clear, they would not cooperate with anything that offended the ill one's personal code. Idiosyncrasies, we call them.

In the past Ralph had refused any help from a male nurse. I knew he was wrong. He knew he was wrong. It was a quirk of thinking from his growing up years. It's so hard to fight an ingrained belief, right or wrong. I told this to the Home Health Service, and no male nurses were ever sent. "In fact," I said, "Ralph requested a pretty, young, and well-shaped female nurse." I laughed, and said a silent prayer for this. Home Health Service sent Marilyn. "A real sweetheart," Ralph called her.

I knew Ralph would not be comfortable with a strange sleep-in male around. Ralph's legs may have been weak, but his will was not. I suspected he would argue and refuse to cooperate with the male helper. Those idiosyncrasies still wanted to be catered to. And when you love someone, and they seem so helpless, you want to please them, to give them some control. Probably, more than anything, he would hate the lack of privacy.

I wondered how I would handle this new problem and still get the job done without offending this fussy husband of mine. If I kept Ralph at home, and he needed to be carried, and I couldn't do it, what choices did I have?

Old friends offered, but the Health Service warned me about having an older man taking care of a disabled one. Would you allow a toddler to carry an infant?

Our youngest son, David, lived only a mile away. He worked full time, had a wife and three children—five-year-old Charis, three-year-old Grant, and three-month-old Alyssa. How could he help me with his father? Even if he were willing, his wife would not like, or feel safe, being left alone at night. Did I have a right to put a strain on their marriage by asking?

Finally I again decided to be honest and blunt, and start with what I most wanted. It had worked all the other times. So I called David. I told him I would understand completely if he said "no." I told him he could back out at any time if he said "yes." I told him his father would have no choice but to accept this situation gradually, as he had others he didn't like. Except now, I thought, there was little time for "gradually." "We're mostly catering to his silly need for privacy," I confided.

David promised to get back to me later in the day, after he consulted his wife, Audrey. Audrey called within a few hours. "How about if we all move in?" Audrey asked. "Then I won't be alone at night, and neither will you."

I cannot explain the relief and joy I felt. Sure, we would be crowded. But love has a way of making room for more.

Talk about catering to idiosyncrasies. That evening David stood in the doorway of his father's bedroom. Ralph lay propped up on pillows.

"Dad," David said. "Can we come and stay in your house while we have our place painted?" It wasn't a lie. In fact they had decided to do just that. I will never forget the smile on Ralph's face. "Sure. I'd be happy to have you."

I wondered how the children's noise would affect Ralph. But he seemed to revel in the lives that filled our small home. When Charis and Grant would peek in the open doorway at him, Ralph would pat the bed. They would quickly climb up and sit next to him. They would stroke his cheek, or touch his arm in a loving gesture. Never rough. They always seemed to know and understand what was going on. We never lied to the children.

What a blessing their stay with us was. We adults did whatever was needed. When David sat on the bed and talked to his Dad, I held baby Alyssa and read to Charis and Grant while Audrey cooked supper. We were all so tired at the end of the day that no one had trouble sleeping. And it was a "good tired."

Acceptance came to all of us. Ralph stopped fighting, and talked a lot about how blessed he had been, how grateful he was to God, and to us. Everyone who cared came to visit. They laughed and joked and teased him, and rarely stayed more than ten minutes, for that was all the strength he had. That was all the time he could stay awake at one time.

Ralph died less than ten days after David and his family moved in. Just as Ralph had been in the next room when David was born, David was in the next room when Ralph died, able to see the wonderful smile on his face, able to touch his father. He was there to say his last good-bye, there to help me in whatever I needed.

Ralph died in my arms, his face looking out at the sunrise. I wish I knew what he saw, what he thought in those last moments. In death Ralph's eyes were open in amazement. His face held a smile. His skin was relaxed, seemed to be younger, smoother.

The cancer had infiltrated his healthy body, but lived a different life. Our objective was to keep the cancer as weak as possible. The treatment worked like chopping away at the parasites from a strong healthy tree.

For eight of his eleven years of cancer we lived an almost normal life—loving, playing, working, traveling. The last three years brought slowing down, staying home, accepting the changes.

The last three months could have been unbearable, but because of our faith, love, and helpful relatives, friends, and paid services, it was not. Acceptance of the unchangeable smoothed those final days.

Strategies

1. Accept the idiosyncrasies of your loved one and if possible, and with honesty, cater to them. Why not make those last days as happy as possible?

2. Accept that when your loved one leaves this world he or she will be safe, pain free, and at peace.

Creative
Meditations

✧ Creative Meditations ✧

May my meditation be pleasing to him, as I rejoice in the Lord.
(Psalm 104:34)

Spiritual master Thomas Merton said, "The important thing in contemplation is not gratification and rest, but awareness, life, creativity, and freedom. In fact contemplation is man's highest and most essential spiritual activity.... It is the awakening of Christ within us, the establishment of the Kingdom of God in our own soul."

This section explains and deals with the uses of creative and structured meditations to enhance your life, and bring you to contemplation.

All these meditations focus inward, toward the imagination. This inward focus is done in order to help a person relax, relieve stress, and find some of the joy Scripture often speaks of.

Each meditation begins with deep breathing. Pictures in the mind are triggered in order to reach a person at his or her core, at the subconscious or unconscious level.

All through the day our minds wander through different levels of awareness. Who hasn't gotten so deeply interested in a book that your flesh jumped when a stranger creaked a door and crept onto the page of the book? Who hasn't drifted into a memory and relived it, sometimes with new understanding? Who hasn't been alert in a card game one hour, and daydreaming a problem to a solution the next? We use a different level of mind to balance our checkbook than we do when we are cooking or teaching our children.

At times I used self-hypnosis to put myself to sleep. This was suggestibility at a deeper level of mind.

We can achieve goals, increase confidence, and enhance our prayer life when we use our imagination and structured meditations. Fantasy and daydreaming are a part of creative activity of the soul.

I suggest that both caregiver and receiver do these exercises, and then discuss what occurred.

Why do we always begin with deep breathing? In the creation of the world everything started with the mighty *ruah* of God (Spirit or wind in Hebrew) sweeping over all the uncontrolled oceans and waters that covered the earth.

It was only when God breathed into man (Genesis 2:7) that man became a living being. As God gave life through breath, you begin each meditation with deep breathing. Deep breathing enriches your body. All functions increase. Shallow breathing keeps you surviving, but deep breathing refreshes, energizes, and increases your thinking. It also decreases toxins as you breath out (expire).

Just as God breathed on the first man, Jesus breathed on his disciples: "And with that he breathed on them and said, 'Receive the Holy Spirit'" (John 20:22). We tune into the power and meaning of our life by deep breathing. Breathing is one of the few bodily functions that can be either deliberate or automatic. When we concentrate on our breathing we focus on the source of our life, and at that moment attention is given to nothing else.

The images that flow through your mind will have a powerful impact on behavior. You must decide what images to allow and which to ignore so the negatives sink and shrink away. Only the positive ones should be allowed to stay.

Longer Meditations (3 to 10 minutes)

✧ Exercise 1 ✧

Enter the Gate
10 minutes

Open to me the gates of righteousness: I will go into them,
and I will praise the Lord: This gate of the Lord,
into which the righteous shall enter.
(Psalm 118:19–20)

To be welcomed into someone's gate is to no longer be a
stranger. You have been invited to pass though the holy gates into
the care of the Lord. For a long time you may have been carrying a heavy burden, a backpack full of fears. When you accept
this invitation to enter the gates of the Lord you will leave your
fears behind. You will rejoice and be glad.

1. Take about five deep breaths and feel yourself relaxing…

2. You carry a heavy spiritual backpack, full of fears. Take a few
seconds to shift this around until it is lighter, not pressing so
deeply into your back…

3. During this meditation you will be traveling a new road….
Look ahead of you to a wide road, easy to travel…

4. Now picture in the distance, at the end of the road, a set of
gleaming white gates trimmed in a soft, almost powdery gold…

5. Walk slowly toward these gates…

6 The closer you get the larger the gates will seem…

7. As you approach can you see the gates slowly opening…

8. You may wish to move faster, but you feel weighed down by

54

your backpack full of fear...

9. Say a little prayer for help...take another deep breath...feel stronger...

10. Shift that backpack around enough so you can pull out a bag. This bag is full of the fear of what others think of you...

11. Give it a form, a size, a weight, a name. Some call this fear "Useless Ego"...

12. You don't need it anymore, do you? Toss it, like a dirty tissue, into the trash can standing beside the road...

13. Take a deep breath and feel how much lighter your backpack is...

14. See and feel how much faster you are moving toward those opening gates...

15. Now from another compartment in your backpack pull out another sack. This sack is full of the fear of failure...give it a form, a weight, a name...some call this "Devil's Drainer"...

16. After examining it, puncture this sack with a prayer, and see it disappear like smoke into the air...

17. Look again down the road to those golden gates, opening wider...how much easier your trip is now...

18. Pull out another bag from your backpack. This one contains your fear of losing what you love...

19. Give what you love a name, and a shape. Look closely at it...Now listen to Jesus' words (John 6:39) that of all which he has given me I should lose nothing...if you give what you love to Jesus you will never lose it.

20. See Jesus walking beside you smiling...

21. Give what you love to Jesus, and he will take away the fear that is loading you down...

22. Feel yourself lighter, moving faster toward those waiting gates...

23. The backpack holds one more package. Take out now this final load...this is your financial fear...examine it closely...

24. How much of this burden can you change? How much can you ignore? How much can you easily handle? Are you doing your best? Give the whole mess to Jesus...somehow Jesus will make it all come out right...

25. Jesus takes your hand and together you can almost fly toward those wide open gates...

26. Enter those gates with thanksgiving and praise, enter and come into your freedom and joy...

27. Take a deep breath and stay in this relaxed and trusting state of God's grace...

28. Ponder these words from Proverbs 3:5: "Trust in the Lord with all thine heart; and lean not unto thine own understanding."

✧ Exercise 2 ✧

Who Am I?
5-7 minutes

Then King David went in and sat before the Lord, and he said:
"Who am I, O Lord God, and what is my family,
that you have brought me this far?"
(1 Chronicles 17:16)

1. Take five deep comfortable breaths…

2. My name is…picture yourself as you are now…

3. My father and mother are…picture them as you remember them. If they are not part of your memory acknowledge this…

4. My greatest spiritual strength is…(choose one or remember one…

5. I remember when I exercised this spiritual strength…(if you cannot find a time, then imagine that you did)…

6. My greatest spiritual weakness at this time is…(pick one, or remember one and acknowledge it)

7. I can overcome my spiritual weakness by…(see yourself acting in a way that would overcome this weakness)

8. My greatest physical strength is…(pick one or imagine one)

9. My greatest physical weakness at this time is…(pick one or acknowledge one)

10. I can overcome this physical weakness by…(see yourself doing something that will help overcome this). One husband said, "Getting my wife to do it." Don't forget to insert humor if you feel like it.

11. My greatest intellectual strength is…(reading, good at num-

bers, understanding puzzles, reasoning, crafts, whatever)...

12. My greatest emotional strength at this time is...(patience, trust, courage). Pick one or imagine one. See yourself acting out or displaying this emotional strength.

13. My weakest emotional response at this time is...(fear of the unknown, lack of control, temper tantrums, judgments without knowledge). Pick one from the list or remember one.

14. I can conquer this by...(see yourself acting in way that will conquer or control this weakness).

15. Ponder these words, from 1 John 3:1: "How great is the love the Father has lavished on us, that we should be called children of God! And that is what we are!"

✧ Exercise 3 ✧

In God's Image
8-10 minutes

*God said to Moses, "I AM WHO I AM. This is what you are to say
to the Israelites: 'I AM has sent me to you.'"*
(Exodus 3:14)

1. Take five deep comfortable breaths and feel yourself relaxing...

2. Remember that I AM is another name for God...I am is also another name for you because God made you...

3. We know much about how good God is. In this meditation we will explore how good you are.

4. Begin by slowly saying, I am...As God's child I am wanted and loved.

5. I am made in God's image.

6. In God's eyes I am beautiful.

7. In God's hands I am healthy.

8. In God's house I am protected.

9. With God's energy I am strong.

10. With God's wisdom I choose rightly.

11. Through God's eyes I am ageless.

12. With God's help I am able to walk and talk in God's realm.

13. With God's grace I am fearless.

14. In God's realm I am able to sing and dance.

15. Because I am God's child I am appreciated.

16. Because I am God's person I am valuable.

17. In God's eyes I am creative.

18. With God's help I am powerful.

19. Because of God I am compassionate.

20. I am a child of God...I am loved...

21. Continue on until you have exhausted all the good things you can think of that you are.

22. Rest in the thoughts of I AM...

✧ Exercise 4 ✧

Sunset
3-5 minutes

*From the rising of the sun to the place where it sets,
the name of the Lord is to be praised.*
(Psalm 113:3)

Sunset is one of the most beautiful times of day. In this meditation you will relax and enjoy the fading glow of God's daylight.

1. Sit in a comfortable position at the time of day when sunset occurs. Face the setting sun, if possible. If not, imagine it.

2. Take about three deep breaths and feel your body relaxing, letting go of the trials of this day...

3. See the changes in the colors of the world as the sun fades...

4. Green turns to gray...shadows cover plants and flowers...

5. Birds begin to settle in...

6. Your eyes may close as you feel drowsy...

7. Can you sense that Jesus is behind you?...

8. Take a few more slow easy breaths as you relax into the end of the day...

9. Like the setting sun your body moves into a new realm for now...

10. Be aware that God is with you...you are safe...you will wake and be alert again when it is time.

✧ Exercise 5 ✧

Jesus Who Rose
8-10 minutes

When Jesus rose early on the first day of the week,
he appeared first to Mary Magdalene…
(Mark 16:9)

The word rose has so many meanings. For Christians probably the most powerful use of it is when we say "He rose from the dead." From this our mind conveys the image of our Lord shining in light and glory—arms out, smiling at us, aglow with a radiance impossible to describe.

The light of Jesus who rose goes from him directly into our heart, our emotions, and we are filled with awe and joy because it is all true. He is the light, the truth, the way. Just as he said.

In the following meditation our loved one that we are caring for will share Jesus' resurrection.

Take about ten deep breaths to relax your body and focus your mind. As you do this murmur the words Jesus who rose as you count down from ten to one.

1. Deep breath…Jesus who rose…
2. Deep breath…Jesus who rose…
3. Deep breath…Jesus who rose…
4. Deep breath…Jesus who rose…
5. Deep breath…Jesus who rose…
6. Deep breath…Jesus who rose…

7. Deep breath…Jesus who rose…

8. Deep breath…Jesus who rose…

9. Deep breath…Jesus who rose…

10. Deep breath…Jesus who rose…

11. Now visualize the risen Christ entering the room where you and your ill loved one are…

12. See the great light emanating from him…

13. See the accepting smile on his face…

14. See his arms outstretched to both of you…

15. Jesus knows all about what is happening to you…Jesus wants you to know that he is part of it…

16. Jesus floats his golden hands over your bodies…as he does this you can sense a light-bodied feeling…

17. Your physical body seems to be separating from your spiritual body…

18. You can see your spiritual bodies begin to float toward Jesus, with no effort on your part…

19. Now both of you stand in full strength next to your Lord and God…

20. Can you feel the slight warmth of his body drawing you closer to him? It is as though he is drawing both of you into him…

21. Now his body begins to rise, and you are rising with him…

22. He takes you with him as you float away from this room…

23. It is as though a gentle wind has picked you up and you are gliding toward the sky…

24. Together you are transported to a garden in a large grass and tree-filled park…

25. The garden is a rose garden…

26. Take a moment to admire the roses…the roses are in all colors and sizes…

27. Now Jesus leads you to a large bush of red roses…

28. Jesus sniffs the roses...and you may sniff the roses, if you like...

29. Jesus lovingly touches a small rosebud, barely showing its red color...it is full of promise...

30. Jesus moves to a larger red rose, fresh open, wound with such beauty...his golden hand caresses it...it sparkles with dew...

31. Leaving this rose, he moves to another, fully opened, slightly tainted with dark around its edges...this red rose he strokes lovingly...

32. Finally he hovers over an old rose, darkened with weather and wind, petals falling, a tired rose...

33. It falls to the earth...tenderly Jesus picks up this rose...

34. He carries it close to his heart, as you all begin to float away from the rose garden...

35. Floating out of the park...Back to the room where you started...

36. Jesus disappears...things seem as they were before he came...

37. Then you see the rose he carried. It is in your room. It is now restored, beautiful, full of red color; dewdrops, like tears, make it sparkle...

38. You know now his feelings for you, his plan for you.

✧ Exercise 6 ✧

Bridge to Heaven
6-8 minutes

Then they heard a loud voice from heaven saying to them,
"Come up here." And they went up to heaven in a cloud,
while their enemies looked on.
(Revelation 11:12)

You are on earth, but you desire more than this. You know life can be better. You just don't know how.

1. See yourself facing a dark corner in the room...

2. Behind you a door opens and a bright light appears...

3. Turn to the light...

4. In the open doorway can you see Jesus?...

5. He beckons to you...

6. You move toward him...

7. His hand is outstretched to you...

8. It seems difficult to get across the room to him...

9. Stretch out your hand to him...

10. Suddenly, as though the distance has been leaped, you are standing next to Jesus...your hands are linked together...

11. Can you feel the pulsing from Jesus' hand which holds yours?

12. Gently now, Jesus tugs you to go along with him...

13. He is turning back to the door, preparing to leave the room...

14. Will you go with him?

15. A sense of peace fills you...

16. Fear is left behind as you and Jesus leave together...

17. Your body seems almost to be floating...

18. Soon you are out into open space...see tall trees and flowers...

19. In the distance is a long broad bridge...

20. Can you see the bridge?...

21. The bridge glows golden in color...

22. The bridge begins at the end of the park area...

23. The bridge expands up into the air, up into the clouds as though reaching to heaven...

24. You and Jesus are gliding toward that bridge, closer and closer...

25. A fearful thought causes you to let go of Jesus' hand...

26. The bridge disappears...

27. You grope again for Jesus' hand...

28. Your hands connect, and the bridge reappears ...

29. Jesus smiles at you...now you know that Jesus is the bridge to heaven...he is the way, the light, the path...

30. Hold on to him and trust...relax...he will transport you safely to heaven.

✧ Exercise 7 ✧

Ten Years Ago
5-7 minutes

*...good news about your faith and love. He has told us
that you always have pleasant memories of us and that
you long to see us, just as we also long to see you.*
(1 Thessalonians 3:6)

1. Sit or lie in a comfortable position and take about three deep comfortable breaths...

2. Allow yourself to sink into a deep state of relaxation, both mental and physical...

3. You will begin to travel back ten years in time. You will do this by visualizing the number Ten...then Nine...Eight... Seven...Six...Five...Four...Three...Two...One...

4. When you reach zero you will feel yourself in an even more relaxed state of mind...

5. You will begin observing yourself as you were ten years ago...

6. You will be seeing only your best self ten years earlier...notice your skin...your hands...as in a mirror, your face...

7. Can you capture for a moment the ten-years-younger you?...the energy...the special interests...

8. Relive for a moment something positive and special that happened to you ten years ago...

9. Was God a conscious part of your life then?

10. If God was a conscious part of your life ten years ago take a moment to review how you knew this, how you interacted...

11. If you were not aware of God being part of your life imagine

now how he was aware of you...how he could have helped you...

12. Imagine now the good things God planned for you ten years ago...(30 sec)

13. Can you see that some of it has happened?...

14. For a moment stay with these images and resolutions of all the good that has come to you in the past ten years...

15. When you are ready, count forward for zero to ten and return to the age you are now.

✧ Exercise 8 ✧

River of Peace
5-7 minutes

Then the angel showed me the river of the water of life, as clear as crystal, flowing from the throne of God and of the Lamb.
(Revelation 22:1)

1. Take five deep comfortable breaths...

2. Just before the sun is fully up imagine yourself standing beside a creek bed...gentle waters flow past your feet...waters deep enough to stand in ankle deep...water cool enough to soothe, but not to chill...

3. Sand lines the bottom of the creek...you may feel troubled, but the waters are not...the water seems determined to make it home to its ocean destination...

4. Watch as calmly, steadily, unceasingly the water makes its way home...it climbs over rocks...it slips over mounds, hills, pressing them lower as it passes downward...

5. Imagine yourself dipping your bare feet into the water...

6. Feel the sand between your toes...these grains of sand that once were a rock...squish your feet around for a while...

7. Feel the flow of the water washing the grime from your feet...soothing them...cooling them...

8. Take a few steps, moving in the direction of the flow...go with the flow...let the waters wash your feet clean...

9. Let the waters carry away your troubles...down and away until they disappear into the ocean...

10. Notice the soothing comfort the water gives to your tired feet as you trudge along...

11. Then you hear the morning bird song, whistling, chirping, singing sweetly…

12. The river has widened, but not deepened…your feet still feel good…

13. As you walk along see a boat sitting along the river bank as though waiting for you to use it…

14. Climb into the boat and let it carry you for a while…

15. Stay with the river. Stay with the boat…but keep alert to the songs, the waving of the trees…the warmth of the sun as it rises from behind the trees….

16. Feel the purity of the wind air as it strokes your face…drops of rain from heaven, these gifts are yours no matter what else is happening in your life.

✧ Exercise 9 ✧

Giver and Receiver
5-7 minutes

*Now we see but a poor reflection as in a mirror; then we shall
see face to face. Now I know in part; then I shall
know fully, even as I am fully known.*
(1 Corinthians 13:12)

Special meditation for caregivers and care receivers:

1. Take about ten deep breaths. As you do count down and image yourself walking down marble steps. One...Two...Three...Four...

2. Hear your footsteps sounding against the smooth marble...Five...Six...Deeper...Relaxed...

3. Seven...Eight...Nine...entering a wide hallway...Ten...

4. There are three corridors leading in three directions...Choose one corridor and imagine yourself entering it and turning a corner...

5. The walls are lined with dark mirrors...

6. As you walk this hallway look into the mirrors...Can you see you are not walking alone...?

7. Behind you is an angel...one of those gifts God promised would always be there to help you...

8. Continue to walk the mirrored hallway...

9. If you look beside you this someone seems not to be there...but in the mirror this person is there...

10. This person is someone who was good to you, a friend, a rel-

ative, a teacher, or a health care person, someone who helped make life easier for you…

11. If you smile at this person, you may see him or her smiling back…

12. Can you remember the greatest thing this person taught you?…think about this for a moment…

13. As you continue your walk you know that if you tire the angel will pick you up and carry you…

14. Can you feel the energy, the strength beyond your own?

15. If you need information or encouragement the person walking beside you, this person who taught you, who helped you, will continue to help…

16. Take another deep breath and stay relaxed as you continue your walk down this mirrored corridor…

17. Now you come to another corridor…turn into it…

18. You have somehow circled around and are back to the marble stairway…

19. As you begin to ascend the stairway, your angel swoops you up and carries you back to where you began…

20. The mirrors are gone…you cannot see your angel, or your special person who taught you…

21. Inside you carry the knowledge that they will always be there to help, to carry you when needed.

✧ Exercise 10 ✧

Caressing Light
4-6 minutes

For my yoke is easy and my burden is light.
(Matthew 11:30)

In this exercise you will need to be barefoot. And it works best if you are lying in bed.

1. Take about three deep comfortable breaths and feel yourself relaxing...

2. Turn your head and shoulders slightly and feel as though gentle fingers are lifting tension...

3. If possible, roll your arms around, releasing any tightness in this area...if you cannot physically do this, imagine it happening...

4. Take another deep breath and relax your arms...now in your imagination lift your hands and, if possible, physically, gently wave them...now wave outward...now wave inward...now in a rolling motion...

5. Now move your hands in a rolling motion as though you are kneading bread, or stirring paint...take another deep breath and enjoy this feeling...

6. Now focus on your feet...visualize your toes, and if possible physically wiggle your toes...now relax them...

7. Now in your mind's eye rub the balls of your feet together, also physically, if you can...

8. Imagine those feet being caressed by gently soothing hands...the toes...the balls of your feet...the tops...

9. Imagine a warm comfortable sensation flowing from your toes, through the tops and to the balls of your feet, and up into your ankles...relax and enjoy this...

10. The tightness is now gone from your head, shoulders, hands, and feet...you feel freer, lighter, more relaxed...

11. Believe God's peace is flowing through you, comforting you...

12. From the top of your head to the tip of your toes your weight is lifted, your tension eased away...

13. Imagine a shadow carrying away toxins from your body...

14. The shadow rises to the ceiling and then disappears into the light...

15. You are left feeling brighter, lighter...relax...stay with these feelings as long as you can.

✧ Exercise 11 ✧

Happiest Dream
1 minute

...your young men will see visions, your old men
will dream dreams.
(Acts 2:17)

1. Can you remember the happiest dream that ever came to you on its own? Think about this for a moment...

2. Can you remember a pleasant daydream you created for yourself? Think about this a moment. Did this daydream ever become a reality?

3. Share these experiences with a person you can trust, a person you care about.

✧ Exercise 12 ✧

Fruits of Your Labor
1 minute

*"Your prayers and gifts to the poor have come up as
a memorial offering before God."*
(Acts 10:4)

The wonder of gifts from God is that unlike material gifts they do
not get used up. Spiritual gifts grow, like a watermelon seed, into
a large vine which bears much fruit.

Your gift or gifts could be some special characteristic you
have, like patience or persistence. Perhaps you have a talent for
working with your hands, or with people. You and the Lord know
what your gift or gifts are. Take a little time and review your gifts
now.

At this time you will review your gift or gifts through the compliments you received from people who benefited.

1. Imagine yourself in some everyday situation and picture someone (it could be someone you know, or it could be a stranger)
complimenting you on your gift.

2. Now see the Lord approaching you...

3. Hear what good things he has to say about how you used your
gift or gifts...

4. Relax and let those compliments fill your soul, like water to a
thirsty tennis player.

✦ Exercise 13 ✦

By the Brook
2 minutes

He makes me lie down in green pastures, he leads me
beside quiet waters...
(Psalm 23:2)

1. Picture yourself in a lovely natural environment, a green open meadow with yellow wildflowers swinging their heads...

2. There is a brook running along the side of the meadow...the air is fresh, caressing you as it breezes past...

3. Near the bubbly brook are some berry bushes...you may pick and eat some whenever you choose...

4. In the distance you can see deer grazing...

5. Sit now by the side of the meadow and relax...

6. The sky is light blue with a few fluffy white clouds...

7. Watch the clouds drift and form into interesting shapes...

8. Breathe deeply of the fresh air...enjoy the beauty and wonder of God's world...

9. As you lie, or sit comfortably, feel free, on vacation from responsibility and troubles...

10. Stay with this, being nurtured by nature for as long as you like.

✧ Exercise 14 ✧

Love Memory
3 minutes

*I think it is right to refresh your memory as long as I live
in the tent of this body.*
(2 Peter 1:13)

1. Take about three deep breaths and feel yourself relaxing...

2. Get into a comfortable position...

3. Remember a time when you felt especially loving toward this person you are caring for...

4. Remember all the details you can about this particular time and incident...

5. Feel the joy you felt then...

6. Feel the love you felt then...

7. Imagine a pink light, and a warm comfortable glow encasing this event...

8. This event is one of your life's treasures...stay with this for a few moments...

9. Let yourself feel rich in love...rich in joy...

10. When you are ready release this memory back to your memory bank, keeping the love and joy as part of your relationship now.

The one cared for should do this meditation as well. The only change being the words "the one you are caring for" to be changed to "the one caring for me."

✧ Exercise 15 ✧

Administering Angel and Your Wish
3 minutes

But during the night an angel of the Lord opened the doors
of the jail and brought them out.
(Acts 5:19)

1. Take about five deep breaths and relax your body...feel it relaxing...

2. Think about your deepest wish, possible or not...

3. Imagine golden doors being opened to you. Beyond those doors is a garden...

4. You, carrying your deepest wish, are being invited to enter those doors, to follow the garden path...

5. When you fix just the right spot, place those wishes down in the golden garden...

6. Walk away, leaving the wishes to God and God's angels to care for.

✧ Exercise 16 ✧

Falling Leaf
30 seconds

*...down the middle of the great street of the city. On each
side of the river stood the tree of life, bearing twelve crops
of fruit, yielding its fruit every month. And the leaves
of the tree are for the healing of the nations.*
(Revelation 22:2)

1. Another simple breathing exercise as you slowly count down from twenty to one...

2. Imagine a leaf falling...

3. See God's gentle hand beneath the leaf, ready to catch it and gently carry it to the ground.

From Darkness to Light
1 minute

...to open their eyes and turn them from darkness to light...
(*Acts 26:18*)

1. Close your eyes, take a deep breath, and accept the darkness for a moment...

2. Now open your eyes forcefully, release your air, clearing away the darkness from you mind and body...

3. Fill yourself with light.

✧ Exercise 18 ✧

Carried by God
2 minutes

*And he carried me away in the Spirit to a mountain great and
high, and showed me the Holy City, Jerusalem,
coming down out of heaven from God.*
(Revelation 21:10)

1. Hope from Scripture. When you tire, imagine yourself being carried by God...

2. Tune into these pictures off and on during the day. It will lighten your load and give you hope.

✧ Exercise 19 ✧

God the Listener
2-3 minutes

*I have seen the affliction of my people...and have heard
their cry...I know their suffering, and I
have come to deliver them...
(Exodus 3:7-9)*

1. Just as the Covenant is for all people in all times, God's promises to Moses in a burning bush apply to all his people in all times...

2. Think of God as the Supreme Listener...use him now. Tell the Lord what bothers you, even though he already knows...

3. Scripture tells us God wants to hear from us, just as a mother whose child is hugging her leg loves to hear those words, "I love you, Mommy"...

4. Address the Lord in your favorite name for him, and begin to tell your concerns...God listens to the words of his people...

5. List your concerns one by one. After each one, wait a bit...listen for his response.

✧ Exercise 20 ✧

Closer to God
2 minutes

A man of many companions may come to ruin, but there is a friend who sticks closer than a brother.
(Proverbs 18:24)

1. Relax your body by deep breathing exercises...

2. Ask yourself the question: what am I doing today to bring my soul closer to God?...

3. Take about ten deep breaths keeping that thought in mind...

4. Then let your mind float...let the answer to that question come to you...

5. Ponder it in all ways...let go and bring your mind back to the outer world.

✧ Exercise 21 ✧

Using my Gifts
2 minutes

*...how much more will your Father in heaven give
good gifts to those who ask him!*
(Matthew 7:11)

1. Take about three deep breaths...

2. Ask yourself the question: how am I using my gifts?

3. Continue to relax and breathe deeply...

4. Let the answers to that question float into your consciousness...

5. Ponder it in all ways...

6. Stay with this as long as you are enjoying it.

✧ Exercise 22 ✧

Names God Calls Me
2-3 minutes

I hope to see you soon, and we will talk face to face.
Peace to you. The friends here send their greetings.
Greet the friends there by name.
(3 John 1:14)

1. Take about three deep breaths and relax…speak to yourself your own name, as you like to be called…

2. Here is a list of names Jesus has called those he loves. How many of these fit his feelings for you?…

> Beloved…
>
> Friend…
>
> Little One…
>
> Child…
>
> Precious…
>
> Disciple…
>
> Faithful one…
>
> Worker…
>
> Helper…
>
> Dear One…
>
> My Own…
>
> Loved One…

3. Listen again until you hear a strong gently voice calling you by one of those names…

4. Relax and carry away from this meditation all the good feelings God wants you to have.

✧ Exercise 23 ✧

Names I Call God
3 minutes

In his name the nations will put their hope.
(Matthew 12:21)

God calls us by name. And we know each other by name. A name is always special and personal. Moses begged God to tell him by what name he should tell the Israelites God is called. And God replied, "I AM" (Exodus 3:15). When the angel Gabriel told Mary of the coming he told her the name for the Savior would be Jesus (Luke 2:21).

In this exercise you will review some of the names for Jesus, and all the special meanings behind those names.

In a slow and easy manner consider each name and what joy this name has brought to you.

1. Take about three deep breaths and relax your body...

2. As you hear the name for Jesus reflect upon how this helped in your life...

3. Jesus, Prince of Peace...have you also been a peacemaker?

4. Jesus, our Strength and our Song...have you also been strength to someone?

5. Jesus, Counselor...have you counseled a troubled one?

6. Jesus, Bread of Life...have you fed and nourished some one in need?

7. Jesus, the Way...have you guided the way of a loved one?...

8. Jesus, Mighty Warrior...when have you fought for someone

you loved and cared for?

9. Jesus, Light of the World…how have you brought light to someone or something?

10. Jesus, Good Shepherd…have I been a good shepherd to those who followed me?

11. Jesus, Living Word…with what words have I helped make the world better?

12. Jesus, Fortress…how have my actions been a fortress to a frightened person?

13. Take a few deep breaths and relax…do you feel a glow? If so, for a few minutes, bask in that glow, that knowledge of some of what you have contributed to the world in Jesus' name.

✧ Exercise 24 ✧

Mantras of Peace
3 minutes

At times I found it impossible to use any techniques to quiet or relax myself. It was then I turned to the sound of my inner song to sustain me. I would simply repeat over and over a short statement that I sincerely believed, and that comforted me. I used many different statements, depending on the occasion. My favorite is this: Jesus is the joy of my life. Whenever I feel like I am getting into trouble, as in traffic, or when my husband, Ralph, was being operated on I used: My Lord leads me through troubled waters.

A friend, whose husband was in the service and serving on a dangerous mission, said that whenever she felt depression coming she repeated, over and over, the phrase: Be with him, O my Lord. She used the tune of "Kum By Ya." It never failed to keep her up and able.

Some suggestions for an inner song, or comforting phrase:

1. Lord, you are love.

2. All things work together for the good of those who love the Lord.

3. You bring only light and truth.

4. My Lord loves peace.

5. My Lord is my joy.

6. You are the God of goodness.

7. You give strength, mercy, and wisdom.

8. My God I trust in you.

9. In your time God, wonders come.

10. Lord, you are the Light and the Way.

Activities
and Games

✧ I ✧

Chit-Chat

Conversational activities for fun and information.

1. Cleverest Person

Name the person you think is the cleverest member of your family and why (only older folks may qualify).

2. Music

Talk about your favorite songs and type of music. Why does this get your toes to tapping and your tongue to humming?

3. Rhyme Games

See how many rhymes you can make from a particular word. Then build a silly sentence around it.

4. Hero

Who is your hero and why? Identify the characteristics that make him or her so in your eyes.

5. Find the Positives

See who can notice what good thing first. This is a great upper, a positive strategy for helping life to be better by being grateful and making it a point to detail and remark about things for which we are grateful.

6. Bible Games

a. *Personalize a passage.* Read a familiar passage and change the words to personalize it. For instance, Judith 13:11: "Our God is with us" to "My God is with me." Or Jeremiah 31:3: "I have loved you with an everlasting love" to "God has loved me with an everlasting love."

b. *Quiz a character.* Pick a Bible character, like David, and learn a lot of little details about him. Then set up a quiz, and later test yourself. Do this for Mary, Martha, etc. Sum up what he or she contributed. What labels fit this character?

How many Marys are there in the Bible? What were the names of the women who stood at the cross with John while all the other men ran away?

c. *Did I know that?* Pick a Bible passage and ask your partner what he or she already knows about it. Then read it, and discuss what is different, what is similar, what surprised you, and what you learned.

d. *Ten Commandments.* Recite the Ten Commandments in order from memory, then check out how correct you were.

7. Clean up Relationships

Mentally clean up your past relationships. In the light of what you now know, do you understand your past angry or confusing actions? Can you forgive? (Work on only one of these at a time. Discuss it until you feel a sense of release or understanding, or release it to another time before you go on to another).

8. Plan for the Future

Play "what if" with the future. What if I owned an acre of land and was planning a flower bed in the front yard—how would I design it? What if I inherited a million dollars—how would I handle it? What if I discovered that I actually....

When any of these become written projects it packs an increased wallop because you can review, append, and change. Insight abounds when writing enters.

✧ II ✧

Lists

1. Female or Male

List all the great things about being female or male. Complete the sentence: It's great to be a female (male) because…

2. Children's Teaching

List all the things children have taught you, especially your own if you have any.

3. Times Spared Disaster

List all the times you were spared disaster, or came through disaster to a better place.

4. Parents Taught Me

List all your parents taught you, beginning with values, cleanliness, control. Progress to games and fun things they introduced you to.

5. Fun Without Money

List all the ways you can enjoy yourself that don't cost money.

6. Simplify Your Life

List all the ways you could simplify your life. Start with stuff you could get rid of and never miss (probably anything you haven't used in three years).

7. Found in the Refrigerator

List all the things you almost always find in the refrigerator.

8. Surprised By

List things you are still surprised by. Start with the way you heat or cool your house, the way transportation has changed, or the way people have surprised you over the years.

9. Right to be Angry

List all you have a right to be angry about (then give the list to God to deal with).

10. Abilities

List all the things you are able to do.

11. People You Love

List all the people you love.

✦ III ✦

Physical Fun

1. Time without Interruption

Give your loved one time without interruption. Without looking at your watch at least for a solid five minutes look into his or her eyes, or directly at his or her face. At least for this time let him or her know he or she is the most important person in your world.

2. Splash Each Other with Water

Best when feet are in a tub of cool water. Takes a bit of toe talent and ankle wiggles. Giggles help, too. If feet are not willing or available, use hands, elbows, nose, or a wet head of hair. Guaranteed to cause laughter. Also works well with a wet towel flung in the direction of other person.

3. Hide the Cheese

Ralph and I had a standing joke about cream cheese. He disliked it and always said, "Don't serve it to me. Don't put that stuff anywhere near me." So one day I found a cartoon about cream cheese and I stuck it in his dresser drawer on top of his underwear. When after a few days he had said nothing, I looked for the cartoon in the drawer. He had left a note saying, "I hid the cheese. Now you go find it." I did, on the bottom of my pile of panties. Then I hid it again in a place he would eventually stumble upon it. And so the game Hide the Cheese began. It was fun to see how long it would take to find that silly cartoon. We never put it in too obscure a place because we wanted it found. We had so much fun with that cartoon, I could write a whole book about that. So find your "cheese" or valentine or fake mouse, and playfully hide it from each other. It keeps a little extra mystery in your lives.

4. Search for a Friend

Search for an old friend. Write him or her a letter whether you find that person or not.

5. Visit a Museum

Visit a museum. Or use an art book borrowed from the library and search the painting for its secret message. What is this painting whispering to you? Make up a short story about what you discovered.

6. Write Silly Poetry

For example:

Roses Are Red
Roses are red, Violets are blue,
I'd probably be lonely, if I didn't have you.

Filled With Joy
Once there was a little boy,
who filled his mother's heart with joy.

He also messed the kitchen and bath,
and incurred the gardener neighbor's wrath.
But, oh, what love he left in his path.

Life's Mix
Life is mixed with good and bad,
Life is mixed with happy and sad,
But whenever I see you, my lad,
I remember the good, and am ever so glad.

7. Armchair Trip

Take an armchair trip to a distant land. Get videos from the library, do a little research, and see yourself going there and doing all the things you want.

8. Paint a Picture

Paint a picture, even if it's paint by number.

9. Sing Songs

Sing songs to each other.

10. Deep Breathing Contest

Have a deep breathing contest.

11. Time Out as a Treat

Be sure to set a private retreat place in your home so that every day you can go there and feel free. It may be the bathroom, or the back porch. Put headphones on and listen to your favorite music. Or read. Or just daydream. Have a special, good-feeling chair or couch. Allow yourself twenty minutes. Settle for no less than ten minutes. This is your space, your place. If guilt creeps in, throw it out by deep breathing and seeing yourself fly away on a golden horse. A bit of pleasurable privacy will replenish your spirit as well as your body. Not only will you feel better, so will those around you.

12. Find a Support Group

Find yourself a support community. There are free caregivers' support groups at many hospitals and almost all senior centers. In this group setting you can say nothing—or say anything—without feeling guilty, and hear things that may help you function better with your situation. It could also provide some social outlet with others in the same situation.

✧ IV ✧

Simple Table Games

All these are easy to learn, usually in one sitting for anyone over eight years of age and understanding. All are usually played sitting in a chair at a table, or sitting up in bed.

1. Dominoes
2. Uno
3. Yahtzee
4. Chinese checkers
5. Aggravation

Aggravation includes dice, marbles, and the board. It has some of the characteristics of Chinese checkers, but with the added spin of jumping on the other's marble and making that player return to the beginning.

6. Skip Bo
7. Activities from a chair
    a) Ring toss
    b) Balls to the bucket
    c) Coin toss to the line
    d) Velcro ball to the target
    e) Bean bag toss
    f) Miniature pool

✧ V ✧

Memory Trips

1. History on Tape

Record personal history on tape.

2. Old Photos

Look at old photos.

3. Music

Sing together the old hymns or songs you once enjoyed. Remember what you can, and playfully make up the rest. This is soothing, brings pleasant memories, and keeps you focused on the moment.

4. Beloved Pets

Discuss the pets you have had.

5. Sports

Reminisce about sports you have enjoyed. Talk about hobbies that brought happiness.

✧ VI ✧

Healing of Memories Exercises

1. First pray for God to walk with you through this hurting time.

2. Now recall an incident that bothered you.

3. Express that original feeling.

4. Change that feeling to a positive one. Start by being glad it's over, and believe that good eventually came from it. You may already know what good came from it. If not, believe that some-day you will understand.

5. Place that memory in a jeweled box. Place it in a storeroom in your mind entitled "Finished Business," and see God filing it away on a shelf.

6. See yourself walking away from that storeroom, away from that memory.

7. Feel satisfied that you have dealt with it as best you can at this time. Review in your mind, and if possible write of these inci-dents. In the ending paragraph sum up how this affected you in a positive way.

✦ VII ✦

Writing
These may be tape-recorded if writing is uncomfortable.

1. Dream Activity

Whenever you remember a dream, write it down, or ask your caregiver to write it for you. After about five dreams, see if a pattern is forming. Are your dreams trying to tell you something? If you haven't a clue, image what they are saying.

2. Make a New Life

Take every road you did not travel and think about it. Then write a story about what would have happened had you traveled that road.

3. A Plan for the Future

Write your ideal future. Plan it. Design the flower bed around your house. See the wedding dress of the next bride in the family. See yourself in a job you love doing.

✦ VIII ✦

Write your Autobiography

Using the following worksheet as a guide, record your personal history.

Autobiography of_____

Date_____

Start by answering the following questions.

1. Vital statistics
Born: when, where, parents' names.

_____

_____

_____

2. Who were the people most important in my life?
When? Why?

_____

_____

_____

_____

_____

_____

3. Which cities, counties, and states have I lived in?

_____

_____

_____

_____

_____

4. What was my education?

_____

_____

_____

_____

5. What jobs have I held?

_____

_____

_____

_____

_____

6. What were my special hobbies or interests?

_____

_____

_____

_____

_____

7. What have I come to believe are my greatest accomplish-
ments?

_____

_____

_____

_____

_____

_____

8. What special experiences changed me? When? Why?

_____

_____

_____

_____

_____

9. What is my medical history, especially times in the hospital,
diseases, or injury that affected me greatly?

_____

_____

_____

_____

_____

10. My philosophy of life is…

_____

_____

_____

_____

_____

_____

Here is a series of additional questions that you may want to use in your autobiography. They pertain particularly to your early childhood, ages one to ten.

1. What was the high point of your early childhood years?

_____

_____

_____

_____

_____

_____

2. What was the best thing you learned during that period, some wisdom that you have used ever since? It could be that you learned you were a valuable person and that confidence has stayed with you and helped you in many difficult decisions.

_____

_____

_____

_____

_____

_____

3. What particular person had the best influence on you during that decade?

_____

_____

_____

_____

_____

_____

    a. What person did you admire the most? Why?

_____

_____

_____

_____

_____

_____

    b. What person taught you the most? Was this a good experience, or just that you took good from it? How were you taught?

_____

_____

_____

_____

_____

4. What did you know during that decade about how your social life influences your decisions? Relate an experience. Did you learn any special social skills (e.g. how to get along with difficult people)?

_____

_____

_____

_____

_____

_____

5. How much did you know about how money influences what happens to you? Give an example. Did you learn any particular money skills? How did your education affect your life?

_____

_____

_____

_____

_____

_____

And here's one final question.

6. What have your healthy life skills been in each decade of your life?

Ages 10-20

_____

_____

20-30

_____

_____

30-40

_____

_____

40-50

_____

_____

50-60

_____

_____

and so on.

_____

_____

_____

_____

_____

_____

_____

_____

_____

Of Related Interest

Suffering Loss, Seeking Healing
Prayers for Pain-Filled Times
Evan Drake Howard

These prayers give guidance and comfort through the various stages of grief and help the aggrieved integrate different kinds of loss in a healthy and positive way. Perfect for those dealing with loss themselves or for pastoral visitors.
699-9, 48 pp, $2.95

Healing Wounded Emotions
Overcoming Life's Hurts
Martin Padovani

A bestseller for over a decade, this book explains how our emotional and spiritual lives interact, and it challenges readers to live fuller, more satisfying lives.
333-7, 128 pp, $7.95

Also on audiobook: (order A-44)
Three 60-minute cassettes, $24.95

Seeking Inner Peace
The Art of Facing Your Emotions
John D. Powers

Through this book, Father Powers helps you get to know yourself better through the process of "inner dialogue." He shows how to come to grips with dormant emotions that cause conflict of mind and soul, and discern what forces within your personality dominate the way you act.
344-2, 112 pp, $8.95

Praying with the Sick
Prayers, Services, Rituals
Sandra DeGidio, OSM

To those who have a strong desire to do something for the sick and suffering, the author offers practical suggestions and an empathetic approach. She offers prayers for: "Someone Who Is Anxious or Afraid," "Someone in Constant Pain," "Blessing for a Premature Newborn," "For a Person Suffering from Addiction or Substance Abuse." A valuable handbook and resource for anyone who ministers to the sick.
893-2, 64 pp, $6.95

Available at religious bookstores or from:

TWENTY-THIRD PUBLICATIONS

P.O. BOX 180 • 185 WILLOW ST. • MYSTIC, CT 06355 • 1-860-536-2611 • 1-800-321-0411 • FAX 1-800-572-0788

Call for a free catalog